FOR A RADICAL LIFE:

MEDITATIONS
BY
DARIA PLATONOVA DUGINA

2024

PRAV Publishing
www.pravpublishing.com
prav@pravpublishing.com

Compiled, Translated and Edited
by Jafe Arnold and John Stachelski

ISBN 978-1-952671-92-0

Foreword

This little book in your hands is, in fact, a great work. It is a grand testimony, an immense endowment, even a matter of life and death. This is because the words that stare back at you and speak to you from these pages belong to Daria Platonova Dugina.

On the night of 20 August 2022, a few months before her 30th birthday, Daria Platonova Dugina was killed in an act of state-sponsored terrorism. Her life was cut short by a car bombing carried out as part of Ukrainian special operations initiated, armed, trained, and funded by the CIA. To this day, the powers-that-be in Kiev and Washington refuse to officially comment — not because they have any issue with taking civilian lives, but because they have, to a limited but still certain extent, realized that they have opened a Pandora's box.

Already at her young age, Daria Platonova Dugina was many and much in one. Among other things, she was an up-and-coming philosopher, geopolitician, political analyst, journalist, activist, artist, and dear friend of many thinkers and activists across continents. She was a profoundly good human being at the same time as her guiding aspiration in life was to become more than human, i.e., to be metaphysical, to be transcendent, to be not only the one who kindles, keeps, and shares a fire, but who becomes the spark and fire itself — herself.

Through the example of her life and death, Daria Platonova Dugina's philosophy, faith, visions, meditations, struggles, and experiences are of incalculable significance to all men and women around the world who seek greater meaning and cause in life, who become radical by choice or by compulsion, who have discovered their path or who still find themselves seeking questions and answers. For veteran dissidents as well as the uninitiated who simply feel that something is wrong not only in, but with the Modern world as a whole, the mind, soul, heart, life, and death of Daria Platonova Dugina offer much-needed nourishment as well as righteous challenge. To understand and learn from Daria Platonova Dugina is one of the rewarding, painstaking opportunities of our time.

For this reason, among many others, we hereby bring forth a unique selection of Daria Platonova Dugina's thoughts and words in the form of this small, portable "handbook" or "quotebook." The words that constitute this mini-volume were drawn from her posthumous philosophical work, *Eschatological Optimism*, her compiled and edited diaries (recently published in Russia under the title *The Depths and Heights of My Heart*), as well as various interviews, articles, and social media posts.

Through these glimpses into her intellect and soul, Daria Platonova Dugina comes to life for you and with you here and now. She becomes a part of your inner and outer dialogue. Even once you slip this booklet back into your pocket or bag, set it down on your desk, bedside or cafe table, or decide to burn it as a sacrificial offering, or offer it as a gift, Daria Platonova Dugina's words have already become a part of your world. With this comes great responsibility. Will you (cor-)respond to her thought and call? Will you (cor-)respond to her life and death? Will you speak and write and act, or will you remain silent? There is no preordained methodology — neither to your response, to the selections of her words presented here, nor to the effects of going through this book and letting Daria Platonova Dugina think and speak aloud.

Perhaps it is first and foremost this completely open possibility — the freedom to receive and to resolve, the challenge to become and be yourself, the call to be someone and something instead of nothing — that Daria Platonova Dugina meant and was meant to bequeath to us and to you. When we write that this little book is, in fact, a great work, a kind of *magnum opus*, it is because behind, throughout, and emanating from this short book is one of the greatest works of all: an authentic, radical, meaningful life with an authentic, radical, meaningful death in mind.

Memento mori.

Amor fati.

— Jafe Arnold

PRAV Publishing

13 January 2024

FOR A RADICAL LIFE:

MEDITATIONS
BY
DARIA PLATONOVA DUGINA

"The feat of the warrior and the feat of the intellectual are inseparable. The intellectual must always be armed, even if he will never use a weapon in practice. The intellectual must first cultivate a readiness to go forth, to step out from the masses and declare a resolute 'No!' to modern civilization."

– "Eschatological Optimism and the Metaphysics of War"
(2021)

"Everyone has their own place in the world, their spiritual Homeland. This is not a purely physical value. Our roots, the origins of our language and our soul are here. There is a spiritual Homeland, and it is our "ours," native and dear to us... But, in some sense, maybe we are all wanderers in truth. This is a very difficult question. What is certain is that wherever we find ourselves in the modern world, we are in the center of hell. It is difficult to see authenticity anywhere. We are cursed. But this is no reason not to rush toward salvation."

– "Eschatological Optimism
and the Metaphysics of War"
(2021)

"We are likely living in the era of the end of the world — this can be seen in the pandemic, in the various natural disasters that have become more frequent, and in the fundamental shifts in politics, geopolitics, and philosophy. After all, what is the point of things like the de-territorialized thinking of Postmodernity or object-oriented ontology!?... In such circumstances, we are in need of the life strategy of eschatological optimism. Eschatological optimism can be a starting point for life, for understanding the meaning of what is happening, for seeking strategies and the motivation to exist. It provides grounds to live with an orientation towards something other than the illusory given reality of the disintegrating and fragmenting world around us."

– *"Eschatological Optimism:*
Sources, Development,
and Main Directions"
(2020)

"The world given to us is not eternal, which means that it has already ended. Eternal is the world of the One, the world of the Good, the world of the Divine, the other world. My will is directed towards the latter."

– *"Eschatological Optimism:
Sources, Development,
and Main Directions"*
(2020)

"Trying to go beyond the boundaries of self, the eschatological optimist, the 'metaphysical frontiersman,' abides in a sphere of at once holding on to the given and casting out towards that which is not, on the border of this world and the one beyond. Such is the structure of the rift — this person's hands are outstretched in both directions: one holds the sky, while one grabs the earth and tries to push off from it."

– *"Eschatological Optimism
and the Metaphysics of War"*
(2021)

"One of the most important characteristics of eschatological optimism is unhappiness. A person who challenges the given, opts for revolt, proclaims a categorical 'No!' and expresses total disagreement with everything surrounding them — such a person is unhappy. After all, they renounce the state in which Nietzsche found the last humans: 'We invented happiness' — say the last human beings, blinking. This person rejects spectacles, entertainment, and refuses to behold the tightrope dancer. They want something else, they challenge the given, and they take a risk, they challenge themselves by directing their will and striking out from within."

– *"Eschatological Optimism
and the Metaphysics of War"*
(2021)

"In any case, I recommend everyone —
philosophers and politicians, beginners as
well as those more experienced — to turn
to the seventh book of Plato's *Republic*
again and again. It would be better to
learn it by heart (preferably in ancient
Greek). If you want to engage in politics
or philosophy, be ready to live a life of
unhappiness. I call this 'eschatological
optimism.'"

– *"The Political Subject
of Populism and the Problem
of 'Unhappy Consciousness'"*
(2018)

"Every *topos*, every place in space, is a point of presence of the emanation, procession, and ascent of eidetic series. The routes of intellectual being in its eternal dimension converge within them. Each focal point is a node from which one can contemplate the whole universe. All political scenarios, the life of society, matters of war and peace, the forms of political structures and cultures, the scenarios of historical events, and their foresight, prediction, and fulfillment are akin to homologous scenarios of the eidetic chains ascending from sensible things to the World Soul, the Intellect, and further to the One as the Good and the One as the ineffable, the Apophatic, Non-Being."

– *"The Political Philosophy
of Proclus Diadochus"*
(2015)

"Within space and alongside the gods, daimons, heroes, and other eidetic entities, the human being is one of the foremost actors of the eidetic, ontological, aesthetic, ethical, and political orders. Neoplatonic political philosophy envisions man as being called to think and act analogously to the gods, to dwell in contemplating the intelligible forms, to attentively peer into the trajectories of earthly events, and to compare them to heavenly scenarios."

– *"The Political Philosophy
of Proclus Diadochus"*
(2015)

"The Earth and its regions, the realms of Land and Sea, are living territories with a sacred topology, all with their own eidetic path through the ages. The human being's task, the human being's political task, is to participate in the Platonic noetic universe on the side of the forces of the higher eidetic series."

— *"The Political Philosophy of Proclus Diadochus"*
(2015)

"For us, truth is the multipolar world, the blossoming variety of different cultures and traditions."

> – *"We Live In The Era Of The End: An Interview with Dari Dougina"*
> (2013)

"The West no longer knows what the state is, it does not know what nature is... In fact, it has committed savage violence against nature... Modern Western man does not understand nature, he destroys it. Modern Western man no longer knows what war is. He deceptively calls for peace and exclaims 'if only there were no war!' But in practice, he cynically provokes the most terrible and bloody wars of all time. In these wars, the human soul is completely annihilated, because when a person fights only out of compulsion, by coercion or for money, they lose the highest meaning of sacred war and become a banal, blind puppet... The modern West does not know genuine war, genuine death, genuine life, genuine existence. It does not know the taste of true being, and it does not know true hierarchy."

– "Eschatological Optimism
and the Metaphysics of War"
(2021)

"It's hard to fight against modernity, but it is surely unbearable to live in it, to agree with the state of things... By fighting for tradition, we are fighting for our deep nature as human beings. Man is not something granted – he is the goal. And we are fighting for the truth of human nature (to be human is to strive for super-humanity). This can be called a holy war... This spiritual war against the (post-)Modern world gives me the force to live. I know that I am fighting against the hegemony of evil for the truth of the eternal Tradition. It is obscured now, but not completely lost. Without it nothing could exist... Our struggle is not only for the ideal human state – it is also a holy war for reestablishing the right ontology."

– *"We Live In The Era Of The End:*
An Interview with Dari Dougina"
(2013)

"After all, a noble being cannot reconcile themself with the conditions of the Kali-Yuga, globalism, and liberal democracy. In all cases, they spontaneously rise up and revolt, even if they do not have the slightest change of victory… In the conditions of the modern world, any stubborn and desperate resistance, any uncompromising struggle against liberalism, globalism, and Satanism, is heroism."

– *"Eschatological Optimism
and the Metaphysics of War"*
(2021)

"War is a key point and moment in the strategy of resisting the world of illusion. It is a challenge to the world, a revolt against it, a desire to subordinate it to sacred will, to saddle it like a force, a stream, and to carry out a coup d'état in the name of higher values."

– *"Eschatological Optimism
and the Metaphysics of War"*
(2021)

"When I, following Evola, pronounce the word 'war,' I have in mind a domain of deep metaphysical revelation. We are talking about war against the dark element, war against the Kali-Yuga... I want to quote Evola once more: 'A warrior tradition and a pure military tradition do not have hatred as the basis of war.' This is very important: true martial tradition does not know hatred. Warriors are genuine peacemakers, people who are filled with love above all else."

– "Eschatological Optimism
and the Metaphysics of War"
(2021)

"There is a difference between ordinary people who are content with their place in being, and philosophers who ascend to the horizon of mystery. When a person turns their gaze from the lower, from the given, from illusion, to the higher, an important change takes place within them — an 'ontological mutation' in Blaga's words. The structure of this person's consciousness changes. The philosopher becomes an ontological mutant."

— *"Eschatological Optimism and the Metaphysics of War"*
(2021)

"Eschatological optimism is the experience of mystery."

– *"Eschatological Optimism*
and the Metaphysics of War"
(2021)

"Genuine politicians and genuine thinkers never find true harmony."

– *"The Political Subject*
of Populism and the Problem
of 'Unhappy Consciousness'"
(2018)

"If we properly think about our finitude, if we acknowledge death, if we cultivate in ourselves a sense of the finitude and illusoriness of our body, and if we think about what is beyond, then we'll discover eschatological optimism within ourselves."

— "Eschatological Optimism: Sources, Development, and Main Directions"
(2020)

"If even one of us, including myself and everyone gathered here today, commits to seeking this 'forest passage,' to becoming the anarch, or to making the strong-willed decision that we must break with the modern world and cultivate the warrior and hero within ourselves, then it seems to me that the world is already saved. Because even a single person can save all of mankind, as we know."

– *"Eschatological Optimism
and the Metaphysics of War"*
(2021)

"A connection with the beyond can be established through anything. Everything has meaning and a higher meaning. Higher meanings are manifest everywhere, and tradition can be found in everything. You only need to have an elevated and active concentration of knowledge of tradition, a verified Traditionalist view, a Traditionalist perspective within yourself to find it... We could say that modern culture is a disputation of principles, a distortion, a twisting, and a reversal — but of what? Of Tradition, that most powerful foundation of all mankind that ensured its survival and flourishing for millennia. Returning to Tradition is not as impossible as it might seem. It is necessary to commit to the 'Turn' of which Heidegger wrote."

– "Eschatological Optimism
and the Metaphysics of War"
(2021)

"The eschatological optimist never waits for an exterior call. They begin their path from the call from within. This is what Heidegger called the 'call of being' or the 'call of conscience'... The call must grow from within. It will never be exterior, outside somewhere, and if it is, then you'll hear it only once you have already heard the call from within. It is like a prophecy. You'll be able to decipher it only once you are innerly ready to decipher it... But one cannot be passive in this regard. You should try to invoke this call through various practices, whether religious, existential, or through the experience of being attentive to the world. If you have no such call, then simply read books, read everyone I've listed today — the Platonists, Neoplatonists, Hegel, Nietzsche, Cioran, Heidegger, Evola."

— "Eschatological Optimism:
Sources, Development,
and Main Directions"
(2020)

"A person begins their return to the source when they ponder how they have already reached the extreme point of matter and how they now need to turn around and begin the process of ἐπιστροφή, that is, ascent to the One. This turn begins the very instant they understand that they have plunged into the illusion to the greatest possible depth. Now they must push off from the bottom, set off, and rise back up. This is where a person commits the rupture of levels by bluntly electing that which is absent instead of that which is present and given... This is where apophatic theology begins. Everything becomes hell and nothing else. But the eschatological optimism does not despair. They entrust their hope to our Lord Jesus Christ."

– *"Athos, the Feminine Principle, Apophaticism, and Eschatological Optimism "*

"Sometimes it is scary where a person can end up in search of enlightenment."

> – "Homo Hierarchicus:
> Tripartite Anthropology
> and the Experience
> of Hierarchical Society"
> (2021)

"Ever since archaic times, the encounter with the sublime has been associated with the experience of trauma. It can lead a human being to death and madness, but it also harbors the possibility of meeting that which lies beyond the human."

> – "The Sublime and the Aesthetics
> of Great Pan" (2021)

"Evil is easy to find and easy to see. In order to see evil, one must go up, not down. Evil is frightening, and what frightens can best be found at the top… When you ascend, moving in the direction of the Absolute, only then do you begin to understand how scary what lies ahead truly is, and how many imperfections within yourself you can find along the way."

*– "Eschatological Optimism:
Sources, Development,
and Main Directions"*
(2020)

"Are things difficult? Yes. Do you want it to be easy? If you answer yes, then you're wrong. Your body can't take it? It can. Dasha, learn to manage yourself properly. Is your nervous tic because of your weak steering? Too many tasks? No, there will always be too many — learn to carry them out. Too hectic? Your fault. Too confusing? You are at war, there are no excuses. Untangle the complex binds. Teach your body to listen to you. Learn to walk fast, don't let yourself down or fly too high. Dasha, if you're no longer here in an hour, then you should live now as if these were your last minutes. Want to sleep? Read! Want to relax? Don't even mention it! Want to take a more peaceful path? Drop it!"

– *Diary, 2019*

"Perhaps the most interesting thing in life is living straightforwardly and strictly whenever everything begins to seem completely pointless. To learn to live without emotions for life. This is the true goal."

– Diary, 10 December 2021

"I am becoming part of a private military company — the 'Terracotta Army.' And if I fail, I'll be betraying my higher Self. Betrayal earns capital punishment."

– Diary, 2019

"The Minister of Defense — that's me."

– Diary, 13 February 2022

"We know that we are sentenced, yet that we won't die, and that we'll never understand each other, we won't learn and we won't be, and that there will be no peace, because we ourselves never came to be… There are no hermitages in a void."

– Diary, 2012

"My maps are not perfect, but their pathways are beginning to pan out… I must become stronger than the laws of the dead closing in on the periphery of the fate of the world."

– Diary, 2013

"Do you know what my only competitive advantage is? That I believe in the end of the world. And that matter is an illusion. The end of the world is, therefore, deliverance. They don't know how far I can go. I am steel."

– Diary, 15 December 2021

"I want to become a source of good in the world. There's nothing more terrifying than this thought."

– Diary, 13 January 2022

"There are people who are like the Minsk Agreements. Their indecisiveness and ineffectiveness are more horrific than war."

– Diary, 2 November 2021

"There are people who are like the Minsk Agreements. They keep war at bay, they cut off their will to the sound of Tibetan bowls that are nothing other than huge factory chimneys and the gigantic lungs of the earth."

– Diary, 2 November 2021

"The only events that can make us come to our senses are radical changes that affect the whole world. War. War is thus the father of things because it makes distinctions and shows the contours of everything. Those which don't correspond to the authentic turn to ashes before a flash of lightning. Those which do, remain. Once you are marked by the flash, what's important is to draw the contours and color in the lines."

– Diary, 24 March 2022

"When being manifests itself, the horizon lights up with a dangerous red sunset. And the land all around (for 1000 km) becomes dead."

– Diary, 29 June 2022

"Power to the imagination! My dreams are like the laws of this world. My melancholy is like the independent principle of all the birds of this country. Understand Tradition. Suffer through the axis of vertical divinity. Create the world like the kings of Hyperborea. In this is the law. Make humanity obey these laws. Make all beings doomed to…"

– Diary, 29 January 2013

"I suddenly felt like I wanted to drop someone in three hits. In principle, I'm capable of doing this. Now I need to learn how to do it in two."

– Diary, 4 February 2019

"When the dead pass away, their earthly energies remain in the world. If you were wise, you could invite them in. If you were very wise, you could embody their will. Arise, o dead!"

– Diary, 17 March 2020

"Learn to see other people. And take their peace."

– Diary, 18 October 2019

"I felt like living a little. And then there was light."

– Diary, 6 November 2021

"A very important discovery: if you don't divide everything into rest/work, then you can become a human being. This dichotomy is a lie. Rest destroys a person, and if there is rest, then there is also work. You must be merciful — charitable — to yourself. Cancel your vacation, then everything will be in harmony!"

– Diary, 13 September 2021

"A very important rule: always, even when you are completely out of energy, at 0, hang on, bend your line....If you hit at a wall with anything — a finger, an elbow, your head, a foot, a spoon, a fork, a blade, a grenade launcher — it'll break at some point. This strong-willed imperative should accompany everything. If a person is ready to break through a wall with their will, then all they have to do is break it with their will and fury. No matter what difficulties lay behind it, you just need to get through it... You just need to put the pedal to the metal, under any circumstances. Dark circles under your eyes don't matter. If you have blood on your hands, keep hitting. If you have a broken finger, poke with another. If your hand is broken, hit with the other. If both hands are broken, headbutt or kick, it doesn't matter. Strike and beat. Nothing else matters. The imperative is will, will, and mind. Let this be the whole of the law."

– Diary, 14 November 2021

"I am a car — a bad, broken, smashed car missing a wheel. And my Super-Self is trying to drive it at 200 km/h. This is correct. It is better than standing in place. Being human means breaking down and overcoming. Being a human is painful."

– Diary, 3 September 2021

"Everything that one wears in culture, as long as a person maintains their vertical existence, as long as they wake up everyday from death, should be overshadowed by some kind of overcoming."

– Diary, 22 November 2021

"When you end up at the point where history is being made, it's a total coincidence. But that's natural, because it was more or less our path."

– Diary, 25 September 2020

"If before everything was 'temporal,' a little battle, now every day is eternity. Eternal. In the sense of the 'event,' *Ereignis*…Thank you for the blockade, it is turning us into Sparta."

– Diary, 28 February 2022

"Knighthood and chivalry now. Flowers now. It's time to live."

— Diary, 2020

"Wherever there is death, there is truth."

— Diary, 2019

"The Sufis have the revolutionary idea of a 'hidden (secret) caliphate,' a supra-state entity unifying an enormous region in the Middle East and Asia and connected with the Naqshbandiya order. Forget, forget, forget, forget... Depart for your hidden caliphate by taking the first book you come across on your shelf and immerse yourself in reading it."

– *Diary, 3 January 2022*

"I want to bury myself under covers and lie in ambush. So that, like a tiger, I might one day leap out and deliver the final blow. Sun Tzu wrote about the importance of calculating every single appearance and step. He also wrote: To win a hundred victories in a hundred battles is not the pinnacle of the art of war. To rout the enemy without a fight — that is the pinnacle. I could live somewhere where there is iron discipline. Tibetan monasteries come to mind. I'll make such a monastery for myself. On nails!"

– Diary, 5 December 2021

"Sometimes at night I dream that I'm howling like a wolf with all my might. Thus howls the soul insulted by the world, deprived of spirit, thrown alone into the world like a silk rag tossed into the outskirts, used to bandage a wound and then thrown away. For dried blood spoils the rag. Sometimes I dream of howling, blood, and a taste drying on my lips in an uncertain, lame step. So that a semblance of eternity in the world of copies would decay and there would be only eternity, which is an instant. Where is my Nietzscheanism? I fall into a rhythm of sentimental, decaying prose. May God let me overshadow it with fire!"

– Diary, 2019

"What do you think: Do you need to cut your flesh every time you utter the word 'I'? I think you should keep your body so that God can descend into it. Like a sculpture, the abbey crowned me: I should manifest God in myself... The body is a ship on which the soul rushes through dark waters."

– Diary, 2019

"I once said that I'm becoming and will become Antigone. Prophecy and recognition are coming to be. I am becoming Antigone."

– Diary, 2 September 2021

"Politics — a form of metaphysical melancholy."

– Diary, 2019

"O doomed ones, how you rush towards the abyss, denying the laws of the Absolute. O, doomed ones! How you pull me into your *proodos*. The vertical waters now flow only downstream. DASEIN HAS REFUSED."

– Diary, 22 December 2019

"Only death awakens and ennobles. Only tragedy gives strength — to the people, to the state, to the lost person. Screams and blood."

– Diary, 14 November 2015

"I think everything proceeds in the very, very right order, so if someone dies — well, this means that such had to be. Of course, it's easier for you yourself to die than to witness death. On the other hand, why are we so afraid of death? We read so much Heidegger and talk about existentials, but when death comes, for some reason we immediately close ourselves off and become little pieces of rust or antifreeze. Why, how can this be? We must march in a broad front with broad stride and furious war cry. Kill, die, accept the dead, bury the dead."

– Diary, 16 October 2020

"I've done a few good things in my life which I won't be ashamed of when I die and present myself for the Final Judgment. The first: I cited René Guénon in a speech at the Council of Europe. That was in 2017, when I was presenting a report on the migration situation in the EU (Russia's perspective, sent by the European department of the Russian Ministry of Foreign Affairs)… I quoted Guénon, and my colleagues shot me a defiant look. But the son of Pallavicini (a Sufi sheikh, Italian dynasty) was there. The sheikh clapped right in the middle of my speech, it was justified. Justified! Like in Aeschylus — 'Justice!' That's my first chest that can count for goodness. The second — I need to concentrate and think. Yet there's no third chest! Because it still needs to be earned before I die. First the chest, then death. Everything in order."

– Diary, 16 October 2020

"Modern culture, through all of its films, trends, and hints, instills in people fear of the other, the mystical. Fearing the dead and trusting the living is an absolutely abnormal position. Our ancestors would be mournful upon seeing such a disposition. The living are more dangerous than the dead — more dangerous, more profane, and stupider."

– Diary, 4 September 2012

"I decide nothing, I never have and never will. All things bear their own signs of fate. I can only choose the boats or ships on which I'll move through life. I have the power to make them magical. I have the power to split the ocean, just like the shores of my hand were once split apart by the smile of a scar."

– Diary, 8 October 2012

"How unpleasant are the egotistical manifestations of every person — everyone! Pettiness, paucity, microscopic horizons, completely incorrect perceptions of the world (even if, in principle, there is no correct one). And how correct is inner contemplation against this backdrop, to immerse oneself in one's inner space, in one's inner horizon — and to work with none other than it. And to go out only so as to carry out necessary communication, in an orderly manner, with a certain protocol for interaction, strictness and, of course, ritual."

– Diary, 22 November 2021

"The real problem, in all likelihood, is that the overwhelming majority of people do not want freedom, or more precisely are even afraid of it. One needs to be free, to become free, since freedom is existence, that is, first and foremost, consciously corresponding with existence along with the unbearable desire to realize it, which is perceived as fate. Then a person is free, yet the world, full of coercion and means of coercion, now serves merely as something revealing his freedom in its full splendor, like how huge masses of primary rock produce crystals under gigantic pressure."

– Diary, 3 January 2022

My sadness is the cry of a Tatar soul, a sandstorm, and the naked steppe. It is the Russian cry and the Mongol yoke. I am completely calm. I am completely calm.

A smooth surface manifests within. The gray color of an even surface.

Gray is the manifesto of thin ice.

Before, I brought the inner deceased out by words, then by tears, now by prayers. Now I'm silent. No one has died inside for a long time, but no one has lived either.

Will is the upholding of tempo, will is the upholding of speed on a road with no cameras, with a smooth gray surface, without clenching when obstacles appear in the way. Will is the imperative.

The inner fire is the coals I won't let go out.

Humidity. Moisture. Rain and rivers. Rivers and lakes draw me in. I'm a person of land who has found herself on the most beautiful fjords.

A smooth surface manifests within. Gray is the color of an even surface. The gray manifesto of thin ice.

The first seven are humility and inculcation.

The second seven are the beginning of the path.

The third seven are will.

The last little ones are *overcoming for their sake.*

– Diary, 29 March 2021

I know not whether I'll ever write a response
To that letter
loud
Like the rolling brooks of a distant land

Unknown and imperishable

A moist word freezes on the lips
like the tear
Of the missus in the sketch by Gustav Klimt

Vertically flow the rivers
Like trees standing guard

And you, glancing at the weed,
Discerned in it the mysterious
firmament and its immortal import

You called it a temple, called it

A Supreme vision

Was that illumination

Or rather sacred ignorance?

In one hall,

On a Dürer painting there sprawl threads
of verdant grass

On the one beside it (through the one)
a hare lies in resignation

The poet and the hero, looking at the
dusty shard of creation

Can make it a little brighter

— January 2018

Russians sometimes sleep
And when they sleep,
Rivers cease to flow.
And clouds freeze.
And sometimes they even tumble
To protect their slumber.
How strange it is
To suddenly fall asleep
To wake up
Then try to grasp
Where sleep is and isn't at hand
And prisons are now asleep
And birds
And asphalt mountains
And houses
And even streets
Trying to stir up from sleep

                   – Diary, 13 November 2021

Yes. By the way. Tomorrow—
Wrap up the stale,
Bid farewell,
Make the sign of the cross,
Give the right to depart,
Come to the monastery,
Seek guidance,
Make a decision — make up your mind,
Then let the dream come true
(phones, of course, disturb sleeping
dreams)

– Diary, 2021

Z

We won

Over waste heaps — the banner flies

By the city in coal dust

We forgot

But the name was a surname — Stalin.

Now we ourselves

Proclaimed

But not alone.

But there are

Problems with watches.

We didn't cancel them

You didn't take them off.

And, we need to admit, we were all late.

— Diary, 12 March 2022

The dead introduced us,

They took compensation in blood,

They took bribes of pain in advance,

They fed on fog and heavenly salt alone

The dead introduced us

Their clocks are glitchy and sleepy

Their pupils are faded and dense

Their breath is like all our seasons spent
together at once

– Diary, 4 April 2019

Lightning will hover over the region,
Dawn will thunder over fields of steel,
Cutting the heavens with his tone
Colonel Light will speak of what is to come

Birds will hover in flocks
The sky will groan in the illusion of sleep.
Over bloody boots
Rises that banner of yours — Spring!

While all the cartridges cut through skin
Breaking through the streams of a new day,
We, gray-haired, sick, rainy,
Shall say to history, 'Yes!'

— Diary, 27 April 2017

This is the deepest, riskiest spiritual experience, and no one knows how it will end... You will struggle when there are no stars, as Christian Hoffmann von Hoffmannswaldau said:

> Up, o Soul, you must learn
> Without stars
> When the weather rages and breaks
> When the black covers of night
> Frighten us,
> To be your own Light for yourself.

> *— "Eschatological Optimism*
> *and the Metaphysics of War"*
> (2021)

"Friends! We are thrown into this world for a short while. We have much to do here. A duty and mission befall us. If we mess up everything, if we senselessly lose ourselves, if we disconnect from this world, if we are lazy, then we won't get far. We need an inner revolution, a revolution of the spirit."

– Diary, 22 November 2020

"Praise be to God that I never died before!"

– Diary, 2020

"Awakening is my crusade."

– Diary, 22 January 2022